WHAT I WANT, WHAT I NEED

"Exploring the Boundaries of Desire and Necessity"

By

Julia Mc'Anney

DEDICATION

This book is dedicated to all those who have struggled to understand the boundaries of desire and necessities in their relationships and career. To those who have searched for love and acceptance, to those who have worked hard to build and maintain meaningful connections, to those who have fought to be true to themselves and their needs. This book is for you, who have the courage to look within, to reflect and grow, to set boundaries and make difficult choices. May this book be a guide and a companion on your journey towards understanding the complexities of relationships and career, and towards attracting positive and meaningful connections in all aspects of life.

DESCRIPTION

"In 'WHAT I WANT, WHAT I NEED,' you are urged to examine the intricate relationship between your desires and necessities. Through engaging personal anecdotes and thought-provoking analysis, this book encourages you to consider the true motivations behind your choices and how they can better align your wants with your needs. Whether you are trying to find fulfillment in your personal or professional life, this book offers a fresh perspective on the age-old question of how to balance what we want with what we truly need."

TABLE OF CONTENT

Chapter 3: *Building and Maintaining Relationships*

- Communication and Trust
- Meeting Needs vs. Following Desires
- Resolving Conflicts and Negotiating Boundaries
- Attracting Long-Term Partners in relationships and career

Chapter 4: *Long-term Commitment*

- Keeping the Spark Alive
- Navigating Change and Growth
- The Art of Compromise.
- Attracting People Who Mean Well in Relationships and Career.

Chapter 5: *Friendship and Platonic Relationships*

- The Different Forms of Love.
- Setting and Maintaining Boundaries.
- Supporting and Being Supported.

Conclusion:

INTRODUCTION

"What I Want, What I Need: Exploring the Boundaries of Desire and Necessities" delves into the complex and often confusing world of love, romance, relationships, friendship and career. This book aims to guide you on how to balance and align your desires and necessities in all aspects of life. Throughout this book, you will be presented with thought-provoking essays and personal anecdotes that will help you understand the nuances of desire and need, and how they shape your interactions with those around you, including your career paths. From the early stages of attraction to the depths of long-term commitment, the book guides you through the various stages of relationships, examining the ways in which your wants and needs evolve and change over time.

This book also examines the intersection of relationships and career, and how to navigate the demands of both in order to achieve personal and professional satisfaction. Whether you're single and looking for love, navigating the ups and downs of a new relationship, or trying to keep the spark alive in a long-term partnership, *"What I Want, What I Need"* offers valuable insights and practical advice for anyone trying to navigate the often-tricky waters of human connection and career fulfillment.

CHAPTER 1

Defining want and need

At its most basic level, a want is something that we desire or long for – something that brings us pleasure or satisfaction. A need, on the other hand, is something that is essential for our survival or well-being. While the distinction between want and need can sometimes be blurry, it is important to recognize that they are distinct concepts.

Understanding the boundaries of desire and necessities is a process of

self-reflection and understanding your own needs and wants. It involves being aware of what you truly desire and what you truly need in different aspects of your life, such as relationships, career, and personal growth. Here are a few steps you can take to understand the boundaries of desire and necessities:

- **Identify your desires and needs:** Take some time to reflect on what you truly desire and what you truly need in different areas of your life. It's important to differentiate between wants and needs, as they can often be confused.

- **Prioritize:** Once you've identified your desires and needs, prioritize them in order of importance. This will help you understand which desires and needs are most important to you and where you should focus your energy.
- **Communicate:** In relationships and career, it is important to communicate your desires and needs to the people you interact with. Clear communication will help you navigate potential conflicts and build trust.
- **Be open to change:** Be open to the possibility that your desires and needs may change over time. Be willing to re-evaluate and adjust your priorities as you grow and change.
- **Seek guidance if needed:** It can be helpful to seek guidance from a therapist or counselor if you are struggling to understand your desires and needs. They can provide you with tools and strategies to help you navigate this process.

Remember that understanding the boundaries of desire and necessities is an ongoing process, and it's important to be patient and kind to yourself as you work through it.

The Importance of Self-Reflection

Self-reflection is an important aspect of understanding the boundaries of desire and necessities. It involves taking time to reflect on your thoughts, feelings, and behaviors, and how they relate to your desires and needs. Here are a few reasons why self-reflection is important:

- **It helps you identify your desires and needs:** By taking the time to reflect on yourself and your life, you can gain a better understanding of what you truly desire and what you truly need.
- **It helps you understand your patterns:** Self-reflection allows you to identify patterns in your thoughts, feelings, and behaviors. This can help you understand why you react to certain situations in certain ways, and how to make positive changes.
- **It helps you make better decisions:** By understanding your desires and needs, you can make more informed decisions about how to proceed in different areas of your life.
- **It helps you improve your relationships:** Self-reflection can help you understand how your desires and needs

may be impacting your relationships, and how to communicate and compromise with others.

- **It helps you in career:** Self-reflection can help you understand how your desires and needs align with your career goals and how to navigate the demands of both in order to achieve personal and professional satisfaction.

Self-reflection is a valuable tool that can help you understand yourself and your life better, and make positive changes. Remember to be patient with yourself as you reflect, and try to approach your thoughts and feelings with curiosity and openness.

Attracting Good and Loving Partners in Relationships and Career

Attracting good and loving partners in relationships and career is an important aspect of understanding the boundaries of desire and necessities. Here are a few tips on how to attract good and loving partners in both aspects of your life:

- **Be confident in yourself:** Confidence is attractive, and when you are confident in yourself, you are more likely to attract good and loving partners.

- **Be clear about your desires and needs:** When you are clear about what you desire and need, it becomes easier to attract partners who align with those desires and needs.
- **Communicate effectively:** Good communication is key in any relationship, and it's important to be able to express your desires and needs in a clear and healthy way.
- **Be open to different types of people:** Don't limit yourself to a specific type of person. Be open to different types of people, as you never know who you might connect with.
- **Show your value:** Show your value as a good partner in relationships and as a valuable employee in career. Demonstrate your skills, knowledge, and worth in order to attract good and loving partners.
- **Be positive and supportive:** People are naturally drawn to positive and supportive individuals, so make sure to be supportive of others and project a positive attitude.
- **Show your authenticity:** Being true to yourself is key to attract good and loving partners. Be authentic, and be true to your values and beliefs.

Remember that it takes time to attract the right partners, and that it's important to be patient and continue to work on yourself and your relationships.

My Thoughts

CHAPTER 2

The Early Stages of Attraction

The early stages of attraction are an exciting and important part of any relationship. These stages are characterized by feelings of excitement, butterflies in the stomach, and a strong desire to get to know the other person. Here are a few things to keep in mind during the early stages of attraction:

- **Pay attention to chemistry:** During the early stages of attraction, it's important to pay attention to the chemistry between you and the other person. This includes physical chemistry, as well as emotional and intellectual chemistry.

- **Be open-minded:** The early stages of attraction are a time to be open-minded and explore the potential of the relationship. Avail yourself to new experiences and new ways of thinking.

- **Communicate effectively:** Good communication is key in any relationship, and it's important to be able to express your thoughts and feelings in a clear and healthy way during the early stages of attraction.

- **Take it slow:** It's important to take things slow during the early stages of attraction. This allows you to get to know the other person better and make sure that the relationship is built on a solid foundation.

- **Be yourself:** It's important to be yourself during the early stages of attraction. Don't try to be somebody you're not, as this will only lead you to disappointment later on.

- **Be open about your intentions:** Be open about what you're looking for in a relationship, whether it's something serious or casual. This will help both parties to understand each other's expectations.

- **Pay attention to red flags:** Be aware of any red flags during the early stages of attraction, such as lack of communication, dishonesty, or disrespectful behavior. It's important to address any red flags as soon as they appear to avoid potential conflicts later on.

Remember that the early stages of attraction are a time for exploration, and that it's important to enjoy the process and take it one step at a time.

The Chemistry of Love

The chemistry of love refers to the complex mix of emotions, physical sensations, and behaviors that are associated with romantic attraction. There are several different factors that contribute to the chemistry of love, including:

- **Hormones:** The release of certain hormones, such as oxytocin and dopamine, can create feelings of pleasure and euphoria in the early stages of a relationship.
- **Pheromones:** Pheromones are chemicals that are released by the body and can play a role in attracting a potential partner.
- **Brain activity:** Certain parts of the brain, such as the reward centers and the amygdala, are activated when someone is attracted to another person. This can create feelings of pleasure and euphoria.

- **Physical attraction:** Physical attraction is an important factor in the chemistry of love. The physical sensations and feelings of pleasure that come from being near a potential partner can contribute to the chemistry of love.

- **Emotional connection:** An emotional connection can also play a role in the chemistry of love. When two people feel understood, validated and accepted by one another, it creates a sense of safety and trust which can lead to deeper feelings of love.

- **Similarities and complementarity:** People are often attracted to those who are similar to them in certain ways, and to those who compliment them in other ways. This can include similarities in values, beliefs, and interests, as well as complementary personalities and life goals.

It's important to note that the chemistry of love is a complex and multi-faceted phenomenon that can differ from person to person and relationships to relationships. It can take time for the chemistry of love to develop, and it's not always a guarantee that the chemistry will lead to a long-lasting relationship.

Navigating the Dating Scene

Navigating the dating scene can be challenging, but it's also an opportunity to explore new connections and possibilities. Here are a few tips for navigating the dating scene:

- **Be clear about your intentions:** Before you start dating, it's important to be clear about what you're looking for in a relationship. Are you looking for something serious, or something casual? Being clear about your intentions will help you find people who align with your desires and needs.

- **Be open-minded:** The dating scene is a time to be open-minded and explore the potential of different connections. Be open to new experiences, new ways of thinking and doing things.

- **Communicate effectively:** Good communication is key in any relationship, and it's important to be able to express your thoughts and feelings in a clear and healthy way during the early stages of dating.

- **Take it slow:** It's important to take things slow when navigating the dating scene. This allows you to get to know the other person better and make sure that the relationship is built on a solid foundation.
- **Be yourself:** It's important to be yourself when navigating the dating scene. Don't try to be someone you're not, it will be difficult keeping up and this will only lead to disappointment in the long run.
- **Be open to different types of people:** Do not limit yourself to a specific type of person. Be open to different types of people, as you never know who you might connect with.
- **Pay attention to red flags:** Be aware of any red flags when navigating the dating scene, such as lack of communication, dishonesty, or disrespectful behavior. It's important to address any red flags as soon as

they appear to avoid potential conflicts later on.

- **Have fun:** The dating scene can be a great opportunity to have fun and meet new people. Always remember to enjoy the process and do not put too much pressure on yourself.

It's important to remember that the dating scene is a process that takes time, and that it's important to have patience and not rush into anything too quickly. Take the time to get to know someone, and don't be afraid to walk away from a relationship if it's not what you're looking for. And remember, not every date or connection will lead to a long-term relationship, but every experience is an opportunity to learn and grow. So, don't be afraid to put yourself out there and enjoy the journey.

Decoding Mixed Signals

Decoding mixed signals can be challenging, but it's important to understand that mixed signals are a normal part of dating and relationships. Here are a few tips for decoding mixed signals:

- **Communicate openly:** The best way to decode mixed signals is to communicate openly with the other person. Ask them directly about their feelings and intentions, and be honest about your own.
- **Look for patterns:** Pay attention to patterns in the other person's behavior. If they consistently give mixed signals, it may be a sign that they're not interested or are not ready for a relationship.
- **Consider the context:** Sometimes, mixed signals can be a result of external factors, such as stress or personal issues. Try to consider the context in which the mixed signals are happening.
- **Be patient:** Decoding mixed signals can take time. Be patient and give the other person space to sort out their feelings.
- **Trust your instincts:** If you feel like something is off, trust your instincts. Your gut feelings are often right, and it's important to pay attention to them.
- **Don't make assumptions:** Avoid making assumptions about the other person's

feelings or intentions. Instead, ask them directly and give them the opportunity to explain themselves.

- **Be honest with yourself:** Be honest with yourself about what you want and what you're willing to accept in a relationship. This will help you to set boundaries and make decisions that align with your desires and needs.

It's important to remember that mixed signals are a normal part of relationships and that everyone can have different ways of expressing their feelings. It's important to communicate openly and be patient when trying to decode mixed signals.

Identifying Red Flags and Attracting Quality People in Relationships and Career

Identifying red flags and attracting quality people in relationships and career is an important aspect of understanding the boundaries of desire and necessities. Here are a few tips on how to identify red flags and attract quality people in both aspects of your life:

- **Pay attention to your gut feelings:** If something feels off about a person or a situation, trust your instincts and pay attention to those feelings.
- **Look for patterns of behavior:** Be aware of patterns of behavior that may indicate a red flag, such as dishonesty, disrespect, or a lack of communication.
- **Be realistic:** Be realistic about what you can expect from a person or a situation. If someone or something seems too good to be true, it probably is.
- **Communicate effectively:** Good communication is key in any relationship, and it's important to be able to express your thoughts and feelings in a clear and healthy way.
- **Be yourself:** Be true to yourself and your values. Attract people who align with your values and beliefs.
- **Show your value:** Show your value as a good partner in relationships and as a

valuable employee in career. Demonstrate your skills, knowledge, and worth in order to attract quality people.

- **Surround yourself with positive people:** Surround yourself with positive people who bring out the best in you. This will help you to attract similar, positive people in your life.
- **Be selective:** Be selective about the people you let into your life. Quality people are often found through referrals from people you trust.

It's important to remember that identifying red flags and attracting quality people is a process that takes time, and that it's important to be patient and continue to work on yourself and your relationships.

My Thoughts

CHAPTER 3

Building and Maintaining Relationships

Building and maintaining relationships is a key aspect of understanding the boundaries of desire and necessities. Here are a few tips on how to build and maintain relationships:

- **Communicate effectively:** Good communication is essential to building and maintaining relationships. Be clear, honest, and open when communicating with others.

- **Show respect:** Show respect for the other person's thoughts, feelings, and boundaries. Respect is a key component of any healthy relationship.

- **Show empathy:** Empathize with the other person's feelings and perspectives. Understanding where they're coming from can help to build trust and intimacy.

- **Be flexible:** Be open to compromise and be willing to make adjustments in order to maintain a healthy relationship.

- **Show appreciation:** Show appreciation for the other person's efforts and contributions. Recognizing the value that they bring to the relationship can help to strengthen the bond.
- **Take responsibility:** Take responsibility for your own actions and be willing to apologize when necessary.
- **Be open to feedback:** Be open to feedback and be willing to make changes in order to improve the relationship.
- **Invest time and effort:** Building and maintaining relationships takes time and effort. Make sure to invest the necessary time and effort in order to keep the relationship strong.

It's important to remember that building and maintaining relationships is an ongoing process, and it requires effort from both parties. It's important to be patient and understanding, and to always strive to improve communication and understanding.

Communication and Trust

Communication and trust are essential components of any healthy relationship, whether it be in personal or professional context. Here are a few tips on how to improve communication and build trust:

- **Be open and honest:** Be open and honest when communicating with others. Honesty is the foundation of trust, and being truthful and transparent can help to build deeper connections.

- **Listen actively:** Listen actively and give the other person your full attention. Show that you're interested in what they have to say and validate their thoughts and feelings.

- **Be clear:** Be clear when communicating your thoughts and feelings. Avoid using vague or ambiguous language that can lead to confusion or misunderstandings.

- **Show empathy:** Show empathy and understanding when communicating with others. Empathy helps to build trust and creates a sense of safety and security.

- **Follow through on your commitments:** Following through on your commitments is crucial to building trust. Keep your promises and be reliable in order to build trust with others.
- **Show respect:** Show respect for the other person's thoughts, feelings, and boundaries. Respecting their boundaries shows that you value and trust them.
- **Be willing to apologize:** Be willing to apologize when necessary and take responsibility for your own actions. Apologizing shows that you value the relationship and are willing to make amends.
- **Be consistent:** Consistency is key in building trust. Be consistent in your actions and words, so that others can rely on you.

It's important to remember that communication and trust are ongoing processes that require effort and patience. It takes time to build trust and strong relationships, but the rewards are well worth it.

Meeting Needs vs. Following Desires

Meeting needs vs. following desires is an important aspect of understanding the boundaries of desire and necessities. It's important to distinguish between what we want and what we truly need in order to achieve personal and professional satisfaction.

Meeting needs refers to fulfilling essential requirements for survival and well-being. These needs include things like food, shelter, safety, and basic human needs such as love and connection. Fulfilling these needs is essential for physical and emotional survival.

Following desires refers to pursuing things we want but don't necessarily need. These can include things like material possessions, status, or certain experiences. Desires can be an important part of our overall happiness, but it's important to strike a balance between fulfilling our desires and meeting our needs.

Here are a few tips on how to balance meeting needs and following desires:

- **Identify your needs:** Take the time to identify your needs and prioritize them over your desires.
- **Be realistic:** Be realistic about what you can achieve in terms of meeting your needs and following your desires.
- **Set priorities:** Set priorities for what's most important to you and make decisions based on those priorities.
- **Be mindful:** Be mindful of your thoughts and feelings as you make decisions about your needs and desires.
- **Communicate effectively:** Communicate your needs and desires effectively to the people involved in your life, in order to avoid misunderstandings and conflicts.
- **Find balance:** Find a balance between meeting your needs and following your desires.
- **Let go of the non-essential:** Learn to let go of desires that are not essential to your well-being, and focus on what is truly important to you.

It's important to remember that striking a balance between meeting your needs and following your desires is essential for achieving personal and professional satisfaction. It's important to identify your needs and prioritize them over your desires, be realistic about what you can achieve, and set priorities for what's most important to you. By being mindful of your thoughts and feelings, communicating effectively, and finding balance, you can achieve a sense of fulfillment and well-being in your relationships and career. It's important to remember that this is an ongoing process that requires effort, patience, and self-reflection.

Resolving Conflicts and Negotiating Boundaries

Resolving conflicts and negotiating boundaries is an important aspect of understanding the boundaries of desire and necessities. Here are a few tips on how to effectively resolve conflicts and negotiate boundaries:

- **Communicate openly:** Open and honest communication is essential when resolving conflicts and negotiating boundaries. Be clear about your thoughts and feelings, and actively listen to the other person's perspective.

- **Show empathy:** Show empathy and understanding when resolving conflicts. Try to see the situation from the other person's point of view, and be willing to compromise.
- **Be assertive:** Be assertive when communicating your needs and boundaries. Speak up for yourself in a calm and respectful manner.
- **Stay focused on the issue at hand:** Stay focused on the specific issue at hand and avoid getting sidetracked by unrelated issues.
- **Be willing to compromise:** Be willing to compromise and find a solution that works for both parties.
- **Take responsibility:** Take responsibility for your own actions and be willing to apologize when necessary.

- **Find a solution that works for both parties:** Find a solution that meets both parties' needs and addresses the concerns of both parties.
- **Follow up:** Follow up on agreements and solutions to ensure that the conflicts have been resolved and boundaries have been respected.

It's important to remember that resolving conflicts and negotiating boundaries takes time, patience, and effort. It's important to be open-minded, willing to compromise, and to maintain effective communication to ensure that the conflicts are resolved and boundaries are respected.

Attracting Long-Term Partners in Relationships and Career

Attracting long-term partners in relationships and career is an important aspect of understanding the boundaries of desire and necessities. Here are a few tips on how to attract long-term partners in both aspects of your life:

- **Be clear about your intentions:** Be clear about what you're looking for in a long-term partner, both in relationships and in career. This will help you to attract people who align with your desires and needs.
- **Show your value:** Show your value as a good partner in relationships and as a valuable employee in career. Demonstrate your skills, knowledge, and worth in order to attract quality people.
- **Build a strong foundation:** Build a strong foundation in your relationships and career by focusing on trust, communication, and shared values.
- **Be consistent:** Consistency is key in building long-term relationships. Be consistent in your actions and words, so that others can rely on you.
- **Be open-minded:** Be open-minded and willing to explore different types of people and opportunities, as you never know who you might connect with.

- **Show respect:** Show respect for the other person's thoughts, feelings, and boundaries. Respecting their boundaries shows that you value and trust them.
- **Be patient:** Finding long-term partners takes time, be patient and don't put too much pressure on yourself.
- **Take care of yourself:** Take care of yourself emotionally, mentally and physically to attract long-term partners who will appreciate and value you.

It's important to remember that building long-term relationships takes time, effort and patience. It's important to be clear about your intentions, build a strong foundation, and be consistent in your actions and words. Showing respect, being open-minded and taking care of yourself will help you to attract the right partners.

My Thoughts

CHAPTER 4

Long-term Commitment

Long-term commitment is an important aspect of any successful relationship, whether it be in a personal or professional context. It requires a willingness to invest time, energy, and resources into building a lasting connection with another person or organization. Here are a few tips on how to make long-term commitment work:

- **Communicate effectively:** Good communication is key to building long-term commitment. Be clear, honest, and open when communicating with your partner or organization.
- **Set clear goals:** Set clear goals for the relationship or partnership and work together to achieve them.
- **Be flexible:** Be open to change and be willing to make adjustments in order to maintain a healthy relationship or partnership.
- **Show appreciation:** Show appreciation for your partner's or organization's efforts

and contributions. Recognizing the value they bring to the relationship can help to strengthen the bond.

- **Make a plan:** Make a plan for how to handle potential challenges and conflicts that may arise in the future.
- **Be willing to compromise:** Be willing to compromise and find a solution that works for both parties.
- **Be consistent:** Consistency is key in building long-term commitment. Be consistent in your actions and words, so that your partner or organization can rely on you.
- **Invest in the relationship:** Invest time and effort into the relationship or partnership. Building a strong foundation takes time, effort, and dedication.

It's important to remember that long-term commitment is an ongoing process that requires effort and patience. Strong relationships and partnerships are built on trust, communication, and shared goals. With the right approach and the right

mindset, long-term commitment can be a
rewarding and fulfilling experience.

Keeping the Spark Alive

Keeping the spark alive in a relationship or partnership is an important aspect of maintaining a healthy and fulfilling connection. Here are a few tips on how to keep the spark alive:

- **Communicate openly:** Open and honest communication is essential for keeping the spark alive. Be clear about your thoughts and feelings, and actively listen to your partner's perspective.
- **Show appreciation:** Show appreciation for your partner's efforts and contributions. Recognizing the value they bring to the relationship can help to strengthen the bond.
- **Make time for each other:** Make time for each other, even if it's just a few minutes a day. Quality time spent together can help to reignite the spark.

- **Try new things:** Trying new things together can help to keep the relationship exciting and fresh. This can be as simple as trying a new restaurant or taking a new class together.
- **Show physical affection:** Show physical affection and intimacy, it can help to keep the spark alive and strengthen the bond.
- **Be open to change:** Be open to change and try new things, it can help to bring excitement and novelty to the relationship.
- **Show interest in each other's lives:** Show interest in each other's lives, it helps to maintain a strong connection and can rekindle the spark.
- **Keep the romance alive:** Keep the romance alive by planning surprise dates, sending thoughtful messages, or planning a romantic weekend getaway.

It's important to remember that keeping the spark alive is an ongoing process that requires effort, patience, and dedication. It's important to make time for each other, try new things and show appreciation for one another. By staying connected and actively working on the relationship, the spark can be maintained and strengthened.

Navigating Change and Growth

Navigating change and growth is an important aspect of understanding the boundaries of desire and necessities. Change and growth are an inevitable part of life, and it's important to develop strategies for dealing with them in a healthy and positive way. Here are a few tips on how to navigate change and growth:

- **Embrace change:** Accept that change is a natural part of life and try to see it as an opportunity for growth and development.
- **Be open-minded:** Be open-minded and willing to explore new opportunities and experiences.
- **Set goals:** Set goals for yourself and work towards achieving them. Having a clear direction can help you navigate change and growth.

- **Build a support system:** Build a support system of friends and family that you can rely on during times of change and growth.
- **Practice self-care:** Practice self-care by taking care of your physical, emotional, and mental well-being.
- **Learn from experiences:** Learn from your experiences and use them to grow and develop as a person.
- **Reflect on your values:** Reflect on your values and make sure that they align with the changes and growth you are experiencing.
- **Be flexible:** Be flexible and adaptable to changes that come your way.

It's important to remember that change and growth can be challenging, but with the right mindset and approach, it can lead to personal and professional growth. Embrace change, be open-minded, set goals, build a support system, practice self-care and reflect on your values, it will help you navigate change and growth in a healthy and positive way.

The Art of Compromise

The art of compromise is an important aspect of understanding the boundaries of desire and necessities. It's an essential skill for building and maintaining healthy relationships, both in personal and professional contexts. Here are a few tips on how to effectively compromise:

- **Listen actively:** Listen actively and give the other person your full attention. Show that you're interested in what they have to say and try to understand their perspective.

- **Communicate effectively:** Communicate your thoughts and feelings clearly and effectively. Be honest and open about your needs and desires.

- **Show empathy:** Show empathy and understanding when communicating with others. Empathy helps to build trust and creates a sense of safety and security.

- **Find common ground:** Find common ground and focus on what you both agree on.

- **Be willing to compromise:** Be willing to compromise and find a solution that works for both parties.
- **Look for win-win solutions:** Look for solutions that benefit both parties and not just one person.
- **Be flexible:** Be open to new ideas and be willing to make adjustments in order to reach a compromise.
- **Follow up:** Follow up on agreements and solutions to ensure that the compromise is being respected.

It's important to remember that compromise is an ongoing process that requires effort and patience. It's essential to be open-minded, willing to listen, and communicate effectively to achieve a compromise that works for all parties involved.

Attracting People Who Mean Well in Relationships and Career

Attracting people who mean well in relationships and career is an important aspect of understanding the boundaries of desire and necessities. Here are a few tips on how to attract people who have good intentions and are genuinely interested in building positive connections with you:

- **Be authentic:** Be true to yourself and let your authenticity shine through. People who mean well will appreciate and respect your honesty and genuineness.
- **Show integrity:** Show integrity by being honest, reliable, and trustworthy. These are qualities that people who mean well will look for in a partner or colleague.
- **Be confident:** Be confident in yourself and your abilities. People who mean well will be drawn to those who are self-assured and have a positive attitude.
- **Show gratitude:** Show gratitude and appreciation for the people who mean well in your life. This will help to strengthen the bond and create a positive environment.
- **Be open-minded:** Be open-minded and willing to explore different types of people and opportunities. People who mean well come from all walks of life and can be found in different settings.

- **Show respect:** Show respect for the other person's thoughts, feelings, and boundaries. Respecting their boundaries shows that you value and trust them.
- **Be consistent:** Be consistent in your actions and words. People who mean well will be able to rely on you and trust you.
- **Take care of yourself:** Take care of yourself emotionally, mentally and physically. When you feel good about yourself, you attract people who will treat you well.

It's important to remember that attracting people who mean well takes time, effort, and patience. By being authentic, showing integrity, being confident, showing gratitude, being open-minded, respectful, consistent, and taking care of yourself, you can attract people who will treat you well in your relationships and career.

My Thoughts

CHAPTER 5

Friendship and Platonic Relationships

Friendship and platonic relationships are an important aspect of understanding the boundaries of desire and necessities. Platonic relationships refer to relationships that are based on mutual respect, trust, and support, without any romantic or sexual involvement. Here are a few tips on how to build and maintain strong platonic relationships:

- **Communicate openly:** Open and honest communication is key to building strong platonic relationships. Be clear about your thoughts and feelings, and actively listen to your friend's perspective.

- **Show appreciation:** Show appreciation for your friend's efforts and contributions. Recognizing the value they bring to the relationship can help to strengthen the bond.

- **Make time for each other:** Make time for each other, even if it's just a few minutes a day. Quality time spent together can help to deepen the friendship.

- **Be supportive:** Be supportive of your friend's goals and aspirations. Offer encouragement and help when needed.

- **Be honest:** Be honest with your friends, and expect the same in return. Trust is essential for a strong friendship.

- **Be respectful:** Be respectful of your friend's thoughts, feelings, and boundaries. Respect their privacy and trust.

- **Be reliable:** Be reliable, if you say you will do something, do it. Show that you can be trusted and dependable.

- **Have fun together:** Have fun together and enjoy each other's company. Laughter and shared experiences are the foundation of a strong friendship.

It's important to remember that friendship and platonic relationships take time, effort, and patience. By communicating openly, showing appreciation, making time for each other, being supportive, honest, respectful, reliable, and having fun together, you can build and maintain strong platonic relationships.

The Different Forms of Love

Love can take many forms and can be experienced in different ways. Here are a few different forms of love that can be experienced:

- **Romantic love:** This type of love is typically characterized by strong feelings of passion and desire. It is often associated with relationships between romantic partners.
- **Platonic love:** This type of love is based on mutual respect, trust, and support, without any romantic or sexual involvement. It is often associated with friendships and other non-romantic relationships.
- **Familial love:** This type of love is the love that exists between family members. It is characterized by a sense of connection and commitment to one another.
- **Self-love:** This type of love is the love that one has for oneself. It is characterized by self-acceptance, self-compassion, and self-care.

- **Divine or spiritual love:** This type of love is the love that one feels for a higher power or divine being. It can be experienced as a sense of connection to something greater than oneself.
- **Agape love:** This type of love is characterized by selflessness, unconditional love, and a willingness to serve others. It is often associated with altruism and charity.
- **Philia love:** This type of love is characterized by deep friendship, affection, and camaraderie. It is often associated with close-knit groups of friends or communities.

It's important to remember that love can take many forms and can be experienced in different ways. Each form of love has its own characteristics and can bring a unique sense of fulfillment and well-being.

Setting and Maintaining Boundaries

Setting and maintaining boundaries is an important aspect of understanding the boundaries of desire and necessities. Boundaries are a way to protect yourself, your feelings, and your personal space. Here are a few tips on how to set and maintain boundaries:

- **Be clear about your boundaries:** Be clear and specific about what you are and are not comfortable with. Communicate your boundaries to those around you.
- **Stick to your boundaries:** Once you have set your boundaries, stick to them. Don't let others pressure or convince you to change them.
- **Respect others' boundaries:** Respect others' boundaries and expect them to respect yours.
- **Communicate clearly:** Communicate your boundaries clearly and assertively, but also be willing to listen to others' perspectives.
- **Learn to say "no":** Learn to say "no" when someone is crossing your boundaries or asking you to do something that makes you uncomfortable.

- **Set healthy limits:** Set healthy limits in order to balance your needs with the needs of others.
- **Take responsibility:** Take responsibility for your own boundaries and do not blame others for not respecting them.
- **Prioritize self-care:** Prioritize self-care and make sure that your boundaries are in line with your physical, emotional, and mental well-being.

It's important to remember that setting and maintaining boundaries is an ongoing process that requires effort, patience, and self-reflection. It's essential to be clear and specific, communicate assertively, respect others' boundaries, and prioritize self-care. By doing so, you can create a healthy balance between your needs and the needs of others.

Supporting and Being Supported

Supporting and being supported is an important aspect of understanding the boundaries of desire and necessities. Support can come in many forms, including emotional, mental, and physical support.

Here are a few tips on how to support and be supported:

- **Communicate openly:** Open and honest communication is key to providing and receiving support. Share your thoughts and feelings with others, and actively listen to their perspectives.
- **Show empathy:** Show empathy and understanding when providing support. Put yourself in the other person's shoes and try to see things from their perspective.
- **Be dependable:** Be dependable and reliable when providing support. Follow through on your commitments and be there for the other person when they need you.
- **Be understanding:** Be understanding when receiving support. Remember that others may not always know the right thing to say or do, but they are trying to help.
- **Be willing to ask for help:** Be willing to ask for help and accept support when you need it. Remember that it's okay to not have all the answers and that you don't have to go through tough times alone.

- **Be supportive:** Be supportive and non-judgmental when providing support. Listen actively, provide encouragement, and offer help when possible.
- **Show appreciation:** Show appreciation for the support you receive. Saying "Thank you" and expressing gratitude can strengthen the bond of support.

It's important to remember that supporting and being supported is an ongoing process that requires effort, patience, and self-reflection. It's essential to communicate openly, be understanding, dependable, supportive, set boundaries, and show appreciation. By doing so, you can create a positive and supportive environment for yourself and others.

Attracting Positive and Supportive Friends in Relationships and Career

Attracting positive and supportive friends in relationships and career is an important aspect of understanding the boundaries of desire and necessities. Here are a few tips on how to attract friends who will be positive and supportive in your life:

- **Be authentic:** Be true to yourself and let your authenticity shine through. Positive and supportive friends will appreciate and respect your honesty and genuineness.
- **Show integrity:** Show integrity by being honest, reliable, and trustworthy. These are qualities that positive and supportive friends will look for in a friend.
- **Be confident:** Be confident in yourself and your abilities. Positive and supportive friends will be drawn to those who are self-assured and have a positive attitude.
- **Show gratitude:** Show gratitude and appreciation for the positive and supportive friends in your life. This will help to strengthen the bond and create a positive environment.
- **Be open-minded**: Be open-minded and willing to explore different types of people and opportunities. Positive and supportive friends come from all walks of life and can be found in different settings.

- **Show respect:** Show respect for the other person's thoughts, feelings, and boundaries. Respecting their boundaries shows that you value and trust them.
- **Be reliable:** Be reliable, if you say you will do something, do it. Show that you can be trusted and dependable.
- **Have fun together:** Have fun together and enjoy each other's company. Laughter and shared experiences are the foundation of a strong friendship.

It's important to remember that attracting positive and supportive friends takes time, effort, and patience. By being authentic, showing integrity, being confident, showing gratitude, being open-minded, respectful, reliable and having fun together, you can attract friends who will be positive and supportive in your relationships and career.

My Thoughts

CHAPTER 6

Career and Professional Relationships

Career and professional relationships are an important aspect of understanding the boundaries of desire and necessities. These relationships can include colleagues, supervisors, mentors, and clients. Here are a few tips on how to build and maintain positive and professional relationships in your career:

- **Communicate effectively:** Communicate effectively and clearly with your colleagues, supervisors, and clients. This can help to build trust and respect.

- **Show respect:** Show respect for others' time, opinions, and boundaries. This can help to create a positive and professional working environment.

- **Be dependable:** Be dependable and reliable in your work. This can help to build trust and respect with your colleagues, supervisors, and clients.

- **Be proactive:** Be proactive in your work and take initiative when appropriate. This can help to demonstrate your commitment and dedication to your job.

- **Network:** Network with your colleagues and professionals in your industry. Building a strong professional network can help you to advance your career.
- **Seek feedback:** Seek feedback from your colleagues, supervisors, and clients. This can help you to identify areas for improvement and to grow professionally.
- **Be open-minded:** Be open-minded and willing to learn from others. This can help to create a positive and professional working environment.
- **Take care of yourself:** Take care of yourself emotionally, mentally, and physically. This can help you to maintain a positive attitude and to perform well in your job.

It's important to remember that building and maintaining positive and professional relationships in your career takes time, effort, and patience. By communicating effectively, showing respect, being dependable, proactive, networking, seeking feedback, being open-minded, and taking care of yourself, you can build and maintain positive and professional relationships in your career.

Aligning Desires and Needs with Career Goals

Aligning your desires and needs with your career goals is an important aspect of understanding the boundaries of desire and necessities. It's important to consider what you want and need out of your career, and how that aligns with your goals and values. Here are a few tips on how to align your desires and needs with your career goals:

- **Assess your values:** Assess your values and what is important to you in your career. This could include things like work-life balance, creativity, or impact.
- **Identify your needs:** Identify your needs in terms of salary, benefits, job security, and work environment.
- **Define your goals:** Define your career goals and what you want to achieve in your professional life.

- **Create an action plan:** Create an action plan for achieving your career goals. This could include things like networking, taking classes, or seeking out mentorship.
- **Keep an open mind:** Keep an open mind about different opportunities and be willing to explore different paths to achieving your career goals.
- **Be flexible:** Be flexible and be willing to adjust your goals and plans as necessary.
- **Invest in yourself:** Invest in yourself by taking classes, attending workshops, or pursuing other forms of professional development.
- **Get a mentor:** Get a mentor who can guide and support you in achieving your career goals.

It's important to remember that aligning your desires and needs with your career goals takes time, effort, and patience. It requires self-reflection and a willingness to explore different paths and opportunities. By assessing your values, identifying your needs, defining your goals, creating an action plan, keeping an open mind, being flexible, investing

in yourself and getting a mentor you can align your
desires and needs with your career goals.

Navigating the Demands of Relationships and Career

Navigating the demands of relationships and career can be challenging as they can both require a lot of time and energy. It's important to find a balance that works for you and to set boundaries to protect your well-being. Here are a few tips on how to navigate the demands of relationships and career:

- **Prioritize:** Prioritize your relationships and career and make sure that you are allocating time and energy accordingly.
- **Communicate:** Communicate your priorities and boundaries with your partner, friends, and colleagues. This can help to ensure that everyone is on the same page and that your needs are being met.
- **Set boundaries:** Set boundaries for yourself in terms of time, energy, and resources. This can help to protect your

well-being and to ensure that you are able to meet the demands of both relationships and career.

- **Be flexible:** Be flexible and be willing to adjust your priorities and boundaries as necessary.
- **Seek balance:** Seek balance in your life by allocating time for self-care and relaxation.
- **Be realistic:** Be realistic about the demands of relationships and career and understand that it is not always possible to have everything in perfect balance at all times.
- **Seek support: Seek support from friends, family, and professionals** when needed.
- **Learn to say no:** Learn to say no when necessary, this can help you to be more selective in your commitments and to avoid over-committing.

It's important to remember that navigating the demands of relationships and career is a complex process and it can require time, effort and patience. By prioritizing, communicating, setting boundaries, being flexible, seeking balance, being realistic, seeking support and learning to say no, you can navigate the demands of relationships and career in a way that works for you.

Building and Maintaining Professional Connections

Building and maintaining professional connections is an important aspect of understanding the boundaries of desire and necessities. Professional connections can help you to advance your career, gain new opportunities, and access valuable resources. Here are a few tips on how to build and maintain professional connections:

- **Network:** Network with professionals in your industry by attending events, joining professional organizations, and connecting with people on LinkedIn.
- **Be authentic:** Be authentic and genuine in your interactions with others. People are more likely to connect with someone who is genuine and sincere.

- **Follow up:** Follow up with people you meet and keep in touch. Maintaining contact is key to building and maintaining professional connections.
- **Offer help:** Offer to help others when you can. This can help to build trust and establish a mutually beneficial relationship.
- **Be a thought leader:** Share your expertise and be a thought leader in your industry by writing articles, giving presentations, or participating in panel discussions.
- **Attend industry events:** Attend industry events, conferences, and trade shows. This is a great way to meet new people and build professional connections.
- **Be respectful:** Be respectful of others' time and resources. Professional connections should be mutually beneficial and not one-sided.
- **Show appreciation:** Show appreciation for the professional connections you have, thank them for their time, knowledge and help.

It's important to remember that building and maintaining professional connections takes time, effort, and patience. It requires networking, being authentic, following up, offering help, being a thought leader, attending industry events, being respectful and showing appreciation. By doing so, you can establish valuable professional connections that can benefit you in your career.

Attracting Positive and Meaningful Connections in Career

Attracting positive and meaningful connections in your career is an important aspect of understanding the boundaries of desire and necessities. Positive and meaningful connections can help you to advance your career, gain new opportunities and access valuable resources. Here are a few tips on how to attract positive and meaningful connections in your career:

- **Be authentic:** Be true to yourself and let your authenticity shine through. Positive and meaningful connections will appreciate and respect your honesty and genuineness.

- **Show integrity:** Show integrity by being honest, reliable and trustworthy. These are qualities that people will look for in a colleague or professional connection.
- **Be confident:** Be confident in yourself and your abilities. Positive and meaningful connections will be drawn to those who are self-assured and have a positive attitude.
- **Network:** Network with people in your industry and attend events, join professional organizations, and connect with people on LinkedIn.
- **Be helpful:** Be helpful and offer your expertise and knowledge to others. This can help establish trust and mutual respect.
- **Show appreciation:** Show appreciation for the positive and meaningful connections in your career. Saying "Thank you" and expressing gratitude can strengthen the bond.
- **Be professional:** Be professional in your interactions and maintain a positive and respectful attitude.

- **Listen actively:** Listen actively and be open to new perspectives and ideas. This can help you to learn from others and to establish positive and meaningful connections.

It's important to remember that attracting positive and meaningful connections in your career takes time, effort, and patience. It requires being authentic, showing integrity, being confident, networking, being helpful, showing appreciation, being professional, listening actively. By doing so, you can establish valuable and positive professional connections that can benefit you in your career.

My Thoughts

_____

_____

_____

_____

_____

_____

_____

_____

_____

_____

_____

CONCLUSION

Embracing the Gray Area

Embracing the gray area is an important aspect of understanding the boundaries of desire and necessities. Sometimes, the line between what we want and what we need is not clear, and it's important to be open to different possibilities and to not have a black and white view of things. Here are a few tips on how to embrace the gray area:

- **Be open to new perspectives:** Be open to new perspectives and ideas, and be willing to consider different points of view.

- **Be flexible:** Be flexible and be willing to adjust your plans and goals as necessary. Sometimes, things don't turn out as we expect, and it's important to be able to adapt.

- **Embrace uncertainty:** Embrace uncertainty and be comfortable with not having all the answers. Sometimes, the gray area is where we learn the most.

- **Be reflective:** Be reflective and take time to think about your desires and needs, and how they align with your goals and values.
- **Consider the bigger picture:** Consider the bigger picture and think about how different options may impact you in the long-term.
- **Seek out different options:** Seek out different options and be willing to explore different paths.
- **Be curious:** Be curious and be open to learning new things.
- **Communicate:** Communicate your thoughts and feelings to others, and actively listen to their perspectives.

The Power of Authenticity

The power of authenticity is an important aspect of understanding the boundaries of desire and necessities. Being authentic means being true to yourself and being honest about your thoughts, feelings, and needs. Here are a few tips on how to harness the power of authenticity:

- **Know yourself:** Take time to understand your values, beliefs, and needs. This will help you to be more authentic in your interactions with others.
- **Be honest:** Be honest and genuine in your interactions with others. This will help to build trust and respect.
- **Speak your truth:** Speak your truth and be open about your thoughts and feelings. This will help to establish healthy boundaries and to communicate your needs.
- **Be true to yourself:** Be true to yourself and don't compromise your values or beliefs to please others.
- **Don't compare yourself to others:** Don't compare yourself to others and don't try to be someone you're not. Embrace your unique qualities and talents.
- **Practice vulnerability:** Practice vulnerability by sharing your thoughts and feelings with others. This can help to build deeper connections and to communicate your needs.

- **Embrace your authenticity:** Embrace your authenticity and be proud of who you are.
- **Embrace change:** Embrace change, be open to learning and growing, and don't be afraid to be different.

The Importance of Self-Care

The importance of self-care cannot be overstated when it comes to understanding the boundaries of desire and necessities. Self-care refers to the actions and practices that individuals take to maintain their physical, emotional, and mental well-being. Here are a few tips on how to prioritize self-care:

- **Set boundaries:** Set boundaries for yourself in terms of time, energy, and resources. This can help to protect your well-being and to ensure that you are able to meet the demands of both relationships and career.
- **Prioritize self-care:** Prioritize self-care activities and make sure that you are allocating time and energy accordingly.

- **Find activities that you enjoy:** Find activities that you enjoy and that make you feel good. This can include things like exercise, reading, or spending time with friends.
- **Take care of your physical health:** Take care of your physical health by eating well, getting enough sleep, and exercising regularly.
- **Practice relaxation techniques:** Practice relaxation techniques such as meditation, yoga, or deep breathing to help reduce stress and anxiety.
- **Seek professional help:** Seek professional help if you are struggling with mental or emotional issues.
- **Connect with others:** Connect with others through social support, whether that's friends, family, or a support group.
- **Be realistic:** Be realistic about the demands of relationships and career and understand that it is not always possible to have everything in perfect balance at all times.

Attracting Positive and Meaningful Connections in all aspects of life

Attracting positive and meaningful connections in all aspects of life is an important aspect of understanding the boundaries of desire and necessities. Positive and meaningful connections can help you to advance your career, improve your relationships, gain new opportunities and access valuable resources. Here are a few tips on how to attract positive and meaningful connections in all aspects of life:

- **Be authentic:** Be true to yourself and let your authenticity shine through. Positive and meaningful connections will appreciate and respect your honesty and genuineness.
- **Show integrity:** Show integrity by being honest, reliable and trustworthy. These are qualities that people will look for in a colleague, friend, or partner.
- **Be confident:** Be confident in yourself and your abilities. Positive and meaningful connections will be drawn to those who are self-assured and have a positive attitude.

- **Network:** Network with people in your industry, join community groups and attend events.
- **Be helpful:** Be helpful and offer your expertise and knowledge to others. This can help establish trust and mutual respect.
- **Show appreciation:** Show appreciation for the positive and meaningful connections in your life. Saying "Thank you" and expressing gratitude can strengthen the bond.
- **Be professional:** Be professional in your interactions and maintain a positive and respectful attitude.
- **Listen actively:** Listen actively and be open to new perspectives and ideas. This can help you to learn from others and to establish positive and meaningful connections.

Conclusion

In conclusion, understanding the boundaries of desire and necessities is crucial to building and

*maintaining positive and meaningful connections
in all aspects of life. It requires self-reflection, setting
and maintaining boundaries, being authentic, and
prioritizing self-care. By understanding and
prioritizing our needs, we can attract good, loving,
and long-term partners, friends, and professional
connections. Additionally, by embracing the gray
area, and being open to new perspectives and ideas,
we can make decisions that align with our goals and
values. It's important to remember that striking a
balance between meeting our needs and following
our desires takes time, effort, and patience. And by
following the tips outlined in this book, we can better
understand and navigate the boundaries of desire
and necessities in all aspects of life.*

My Thoughts

My Thoughts